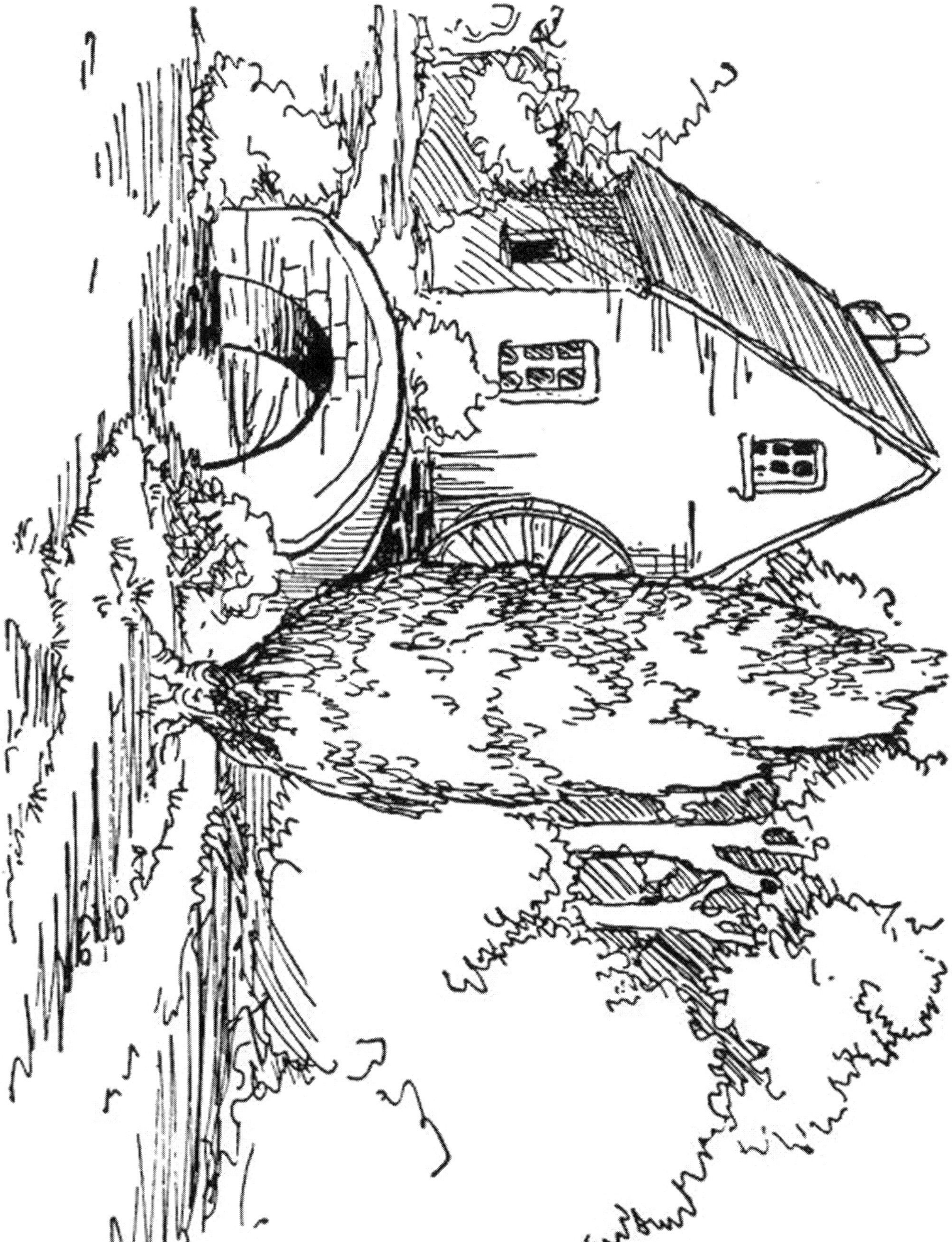

to camp

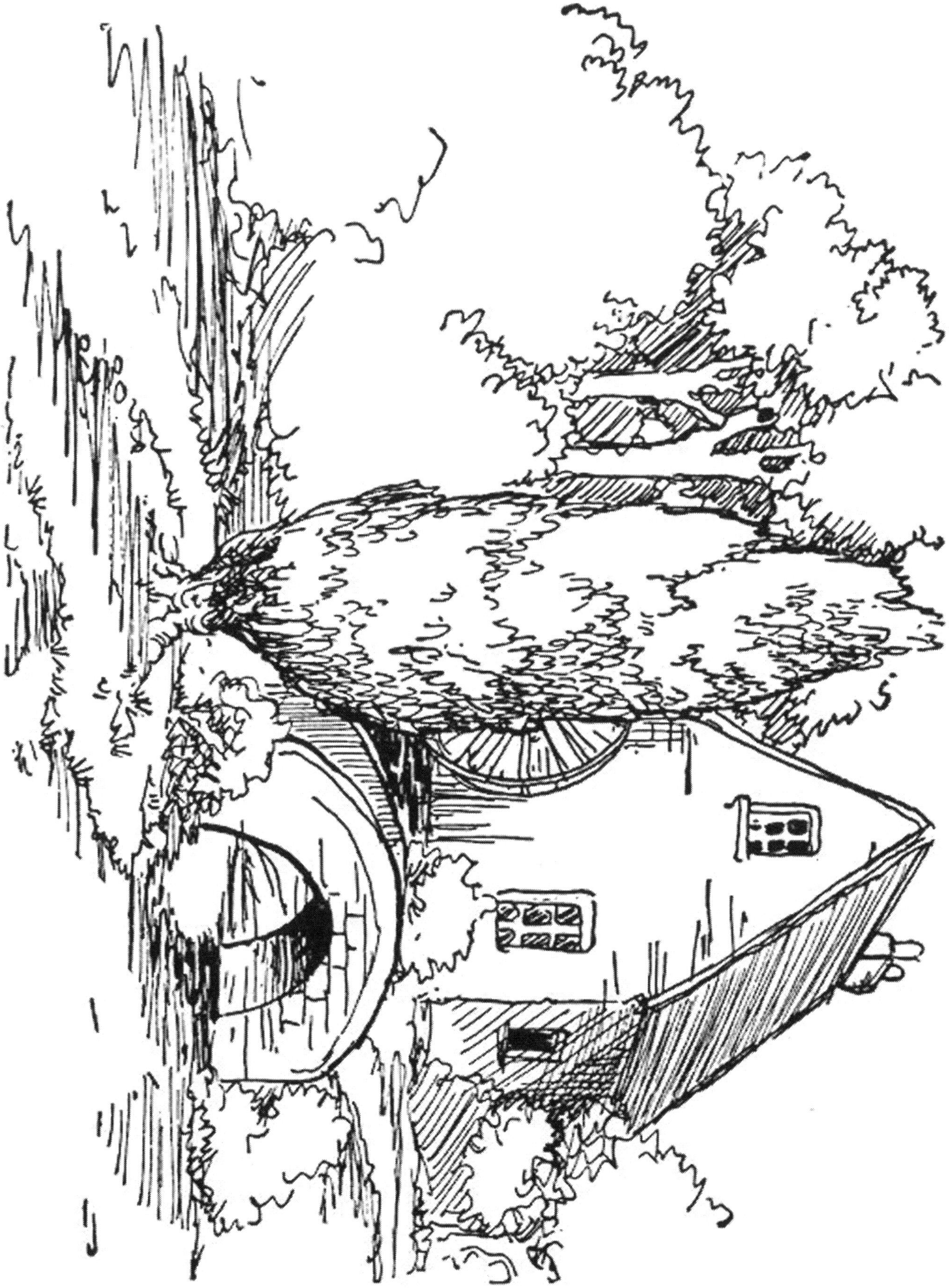

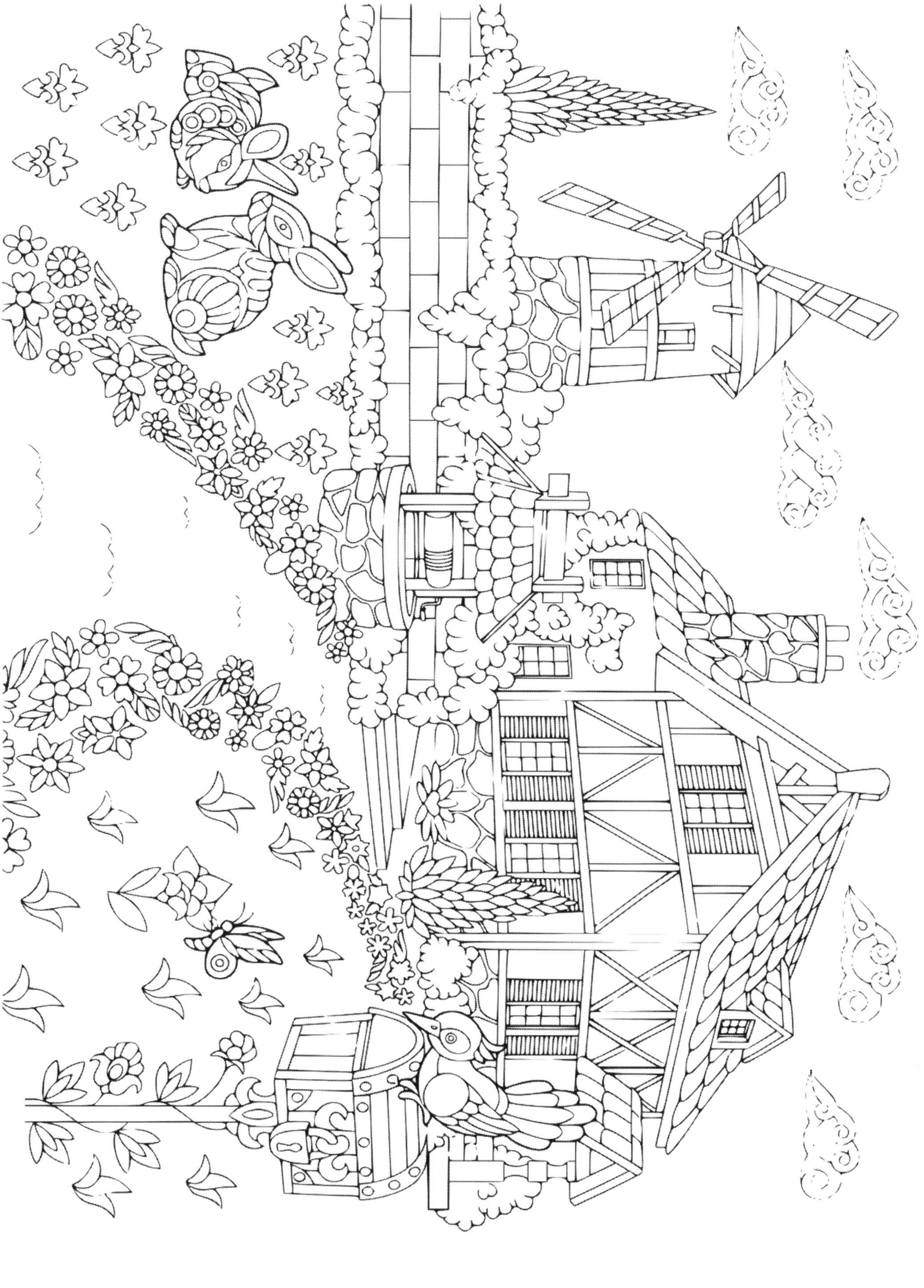

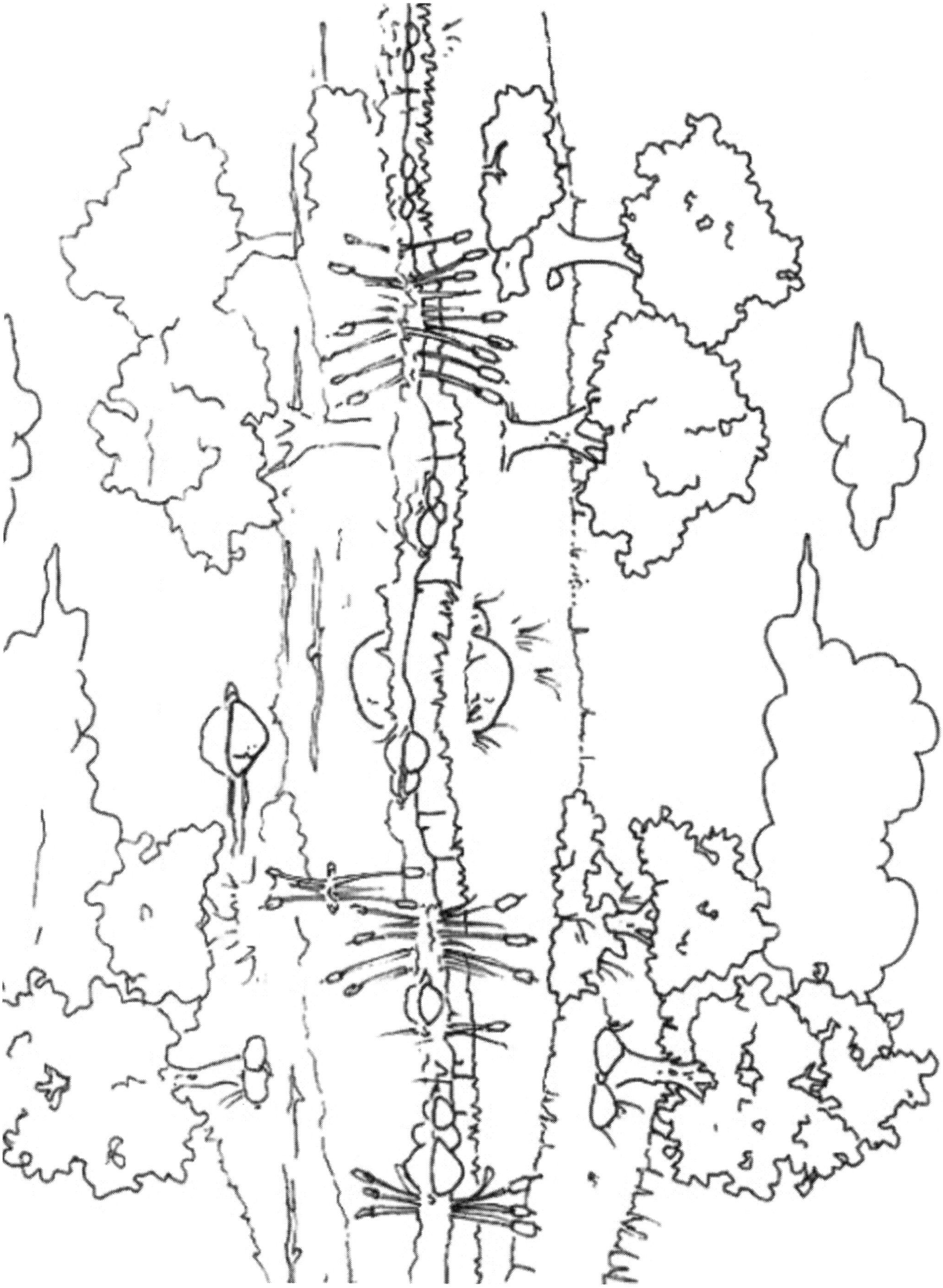

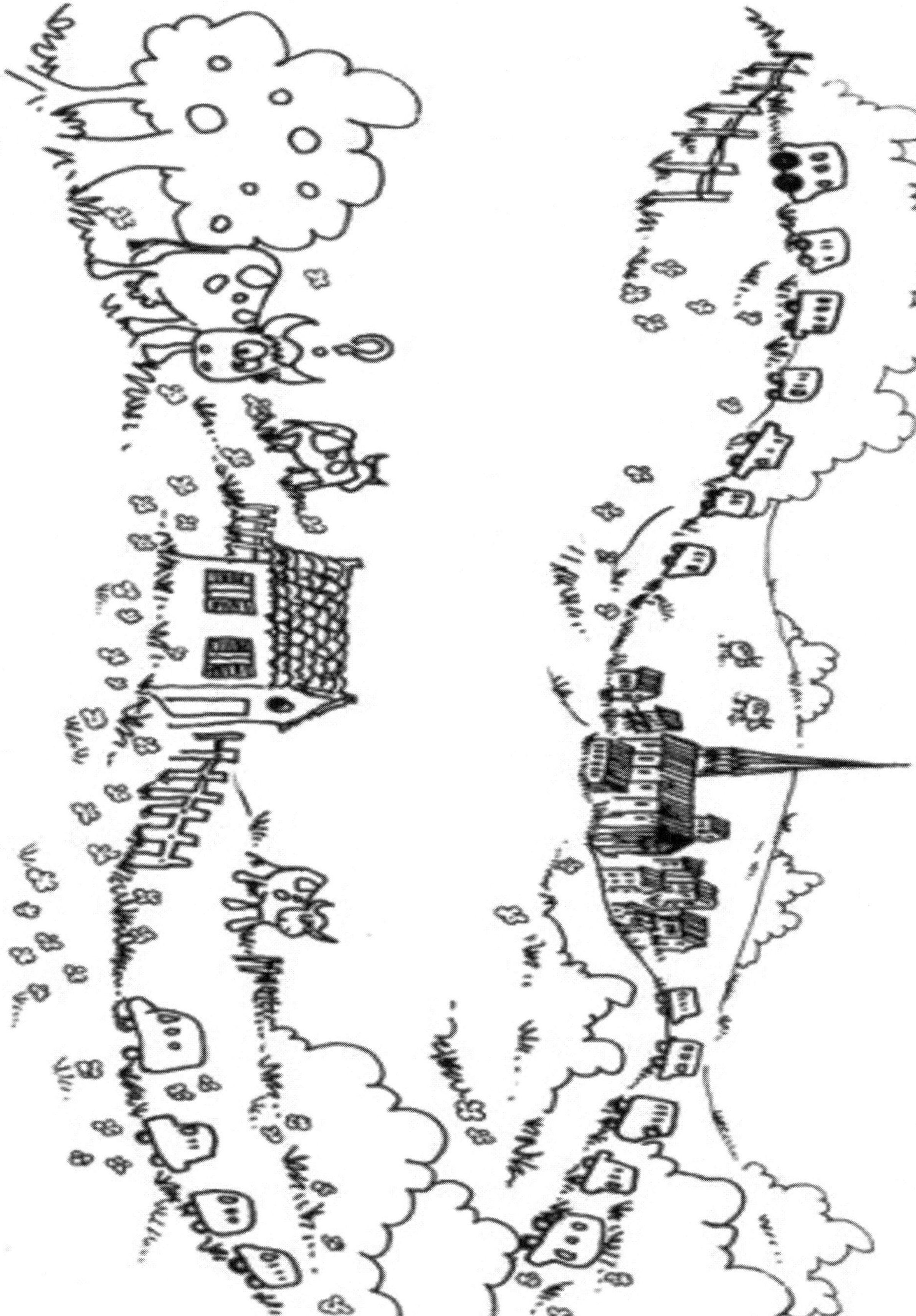

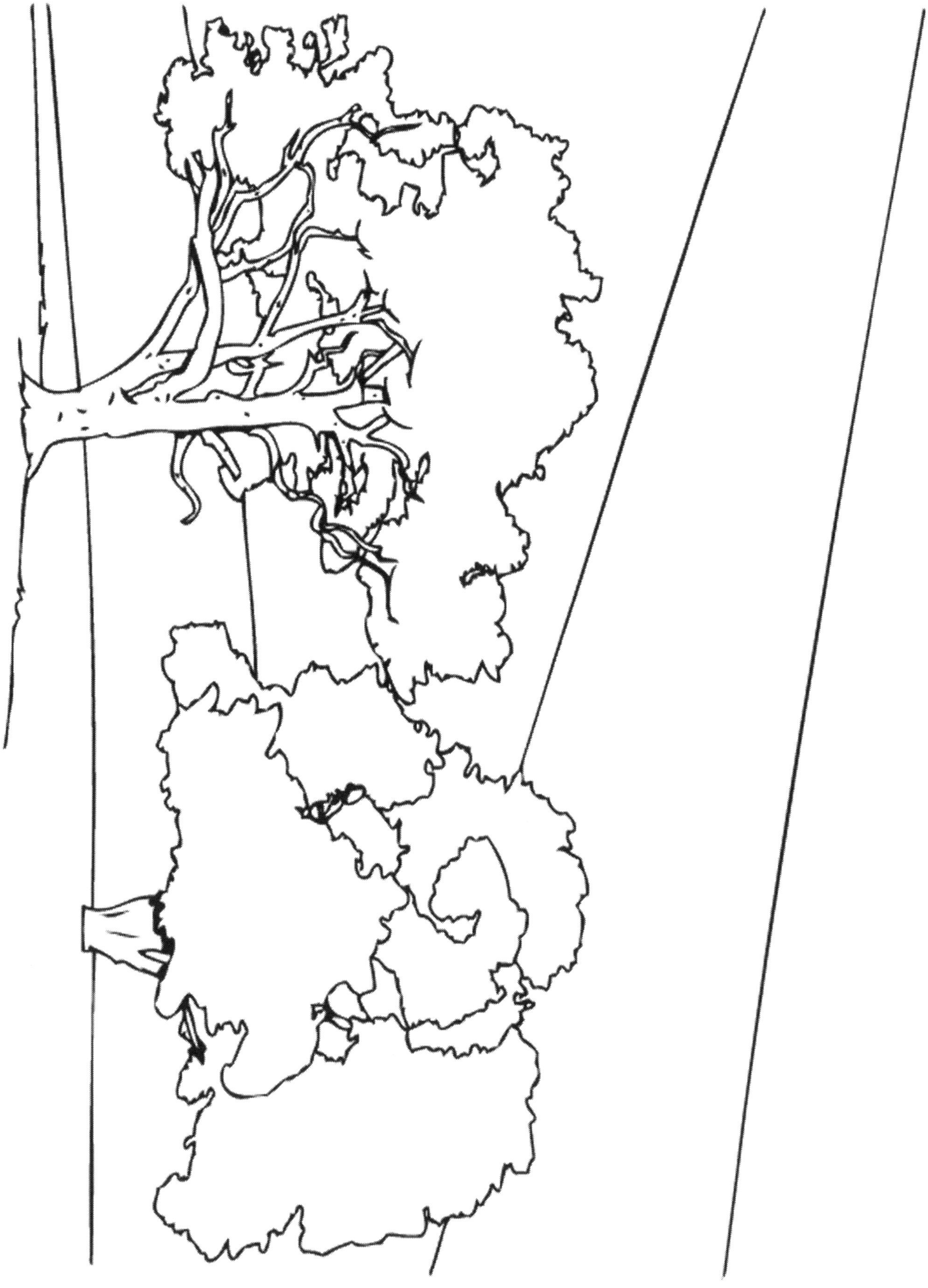

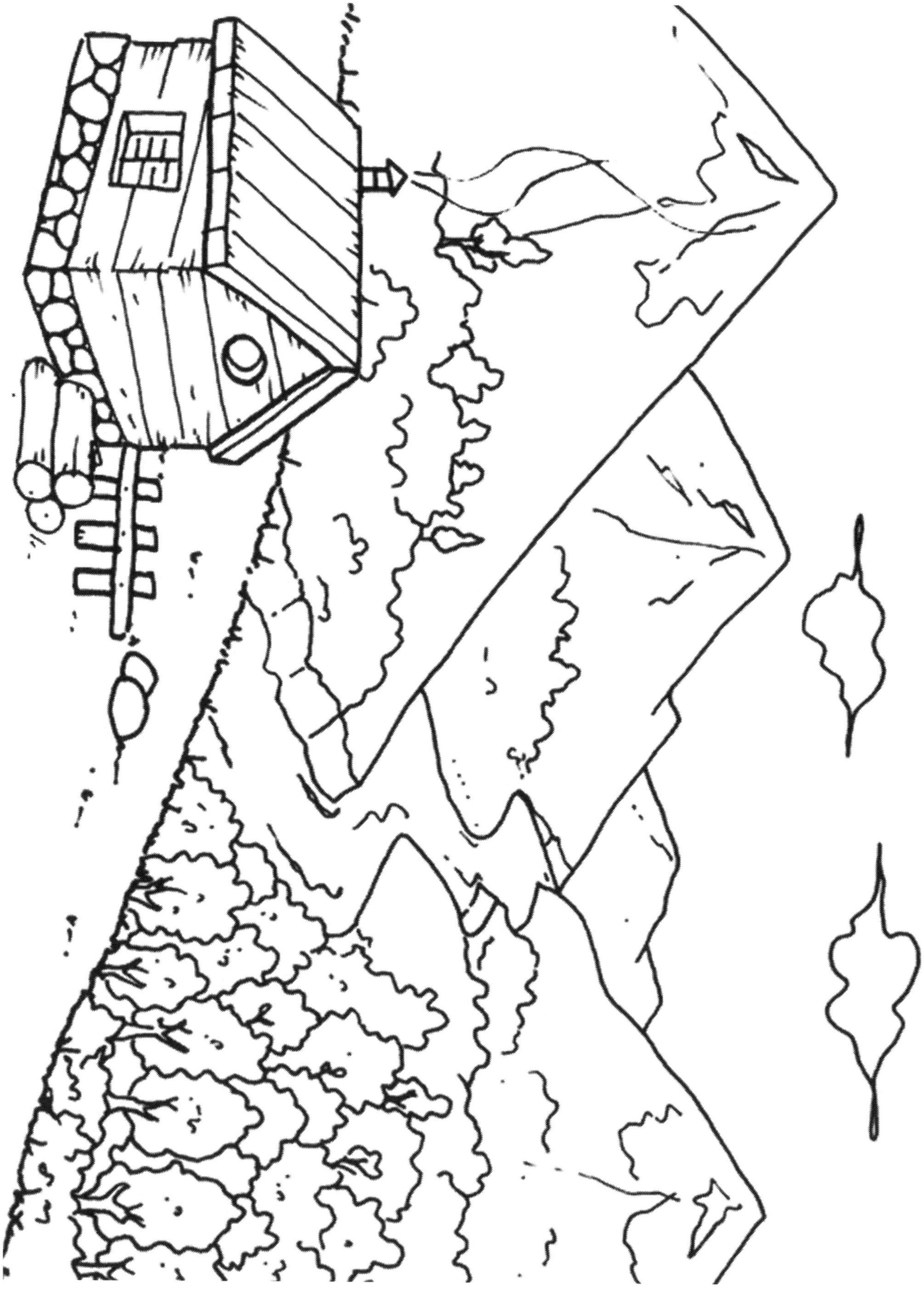

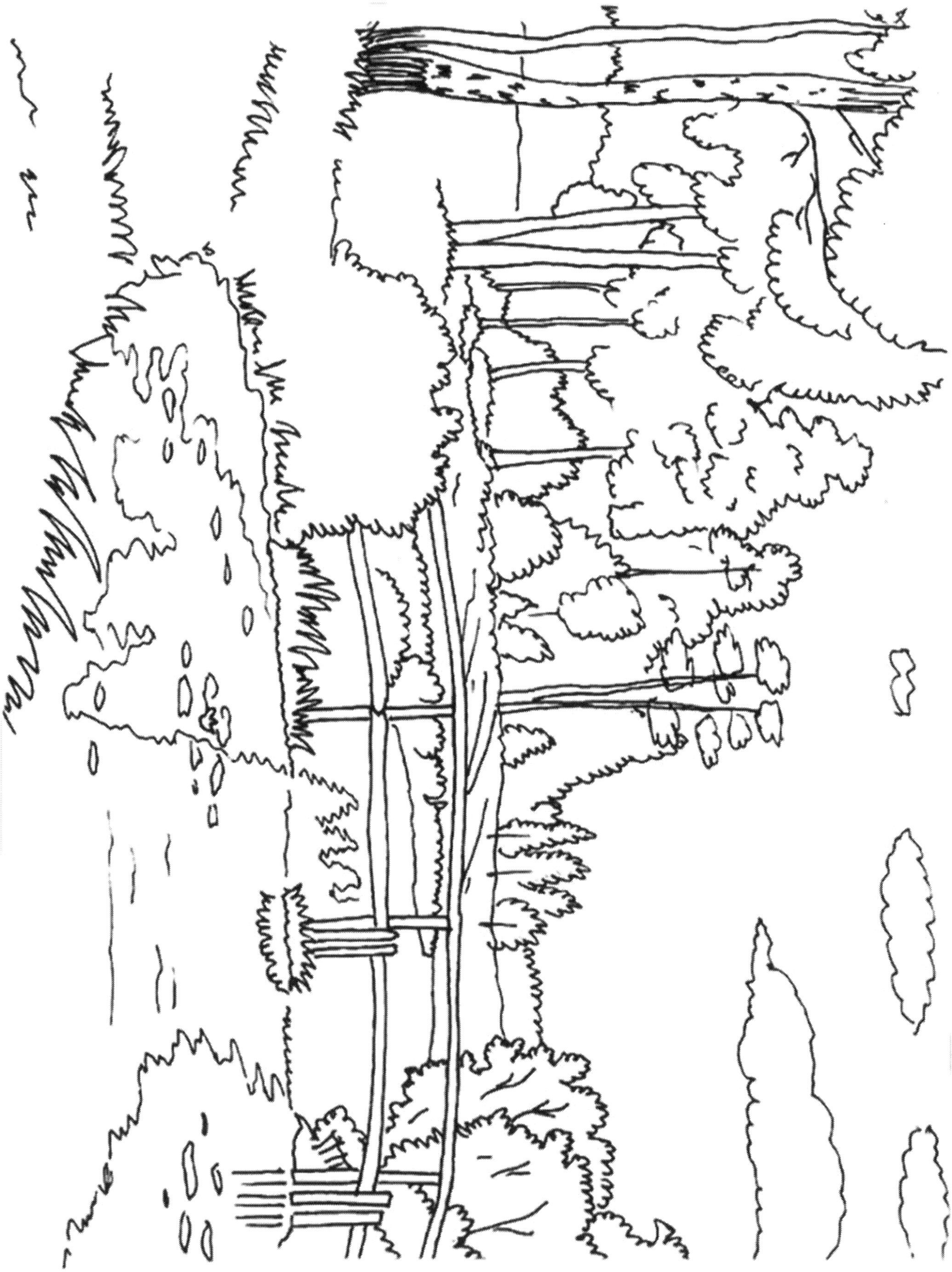

Made in the USA
Columbia, SC
20 September 2023

23110845R10057